C000070384

# Colour

## Living with and loving it

TAVERNE AGENCY

## TERRA

## THE AUTHORS

As the founder of Taverne Agency, **Nathalie Taverne** has spent the past eleven years working with the world's finest interior, lifestyle and food photographers, ensuring their work appears in the world's finest magazines. Within the Taverne collection, original and inspirational homes from around the world are brought together under one roof, with the stories of those who design and live in them as fascinating as the photographs are beautiful. Nathalie and her husband and business partner Robert Borghuis live and work in Amsterdam and together find time to raise their two children, Elena and John.

Having begun her writing career on the *Financial Times*' award-winning *How To Spend It* magazine, **Anna Lambert** went on to spend three years working in the Netherlands, where she met and started working with Nathalie Taverne. Anna's work has appeared in interiors magazines worldwide, including *Australian Vogue Living*, *World of Interiors*, *Elle Decoration* and *Elle Wonen*, and she is the author of *Easy Living*, *Inspirational Apartments* and, with Nathalie Taverne, of *The Natural Home*, *Vintage Living* and *Small Homes*, all published by Terra Lannoo. She lives with her husband and two daughters in the UK.

© 2011 Uitgeverij Terra Lannoo B.V.
P.O. Box 614, 6800 AP Arnhem
The Netherlands
info@terralannoo.nl
www.terralannoo.nl
Uitgeverij Terra is part of the Lannoo group, Belgium

Text and images: © 2011 Taverne Agency B.V.
Lisdoddelaan 79
1087 KB Amsterdam
The Netherlands
www.taverneagency.com

Compilation: Nathalie Taverne
Text: Anna Lambert
Design: Ben Lambers, Studio Aandacht
Printed and bound: Leo Paper Products Ltd., Hongkong

ISBN 978 90 8989 281 2
NUR 454
Also published in Dutch as *Kleur*
(ISBN 978 90 8989 280 5)

No part of this publication may be reproduced or transmitted in any form or by any means, electronic or mechanical, including photography, recording or any other storage and retrieval system, without prior permission in writing from the publisher.

# A colourful life

**As anyone who has ever felt uplifted when adding a bright pink scarf to a black coat, or admired a cerulean blue sky on a summer's day will confirm, we're all influenced by colour. And how we respond to various shades will have a tremendous impact on how we feel within our own homes.**

One of the best things about introducing colour into your home is that to do so is a relatively inexpensive and simple procedure – in an average-sized space, you really can paint a feature wall in a striking shade in less than an afternoon. Alternatively, cushions, fabrics and blinds are all good ways of introducing your favourite tones into a room. With colour, you can be as experimental as you like – and that's one of the things that makes it the ultimate home-enhancer. In the pages that follow, you'll find every sort of space in every sort of colour. In creating homes that suit their tastes and lifestyles, their owners have let nothing hold them back – let them inspire you and, when it comes to using the colours you love in your own home, don't let anything hold you back, either!

# Blue
# tones

**One of the things that makes colour so exciting to work with is the way in which it evokes different responses in different people – and tones that fall within the blue spectrum are certainly no exception. To some, the clarity and natural connotations of blue – blue skies, the sea – mean it resonates as a shade of openness and freedom, redolent of the vast expanses to be found within the natural world.**

Others see blue as a mysterious, velvety colour – think of midnight, or the blue folds of Christ's and the Virgin Mary's robes. It has luxury connotations, too: the first deep and rich shades of blue, made as they were from crushed lapis lazuli, were as costly to produce as they were beautiful to look at. When fading to grey, however, blue can be perceived as a cold, drab colour; depressed Americans even refer to 'feeling blue'. Blue can, of course, be all of these things and none of them. What is a given, though, is that it's a colour that's particularly affected by the natural light it's surrounded by. That's why, in colder, northern-European light, many home-makers avoid it as a shade within living rooms, simply because it lacks warmth. In hotter climates, though, the brighter light gives blue a richer appearance, and

it has a practical application, too: in Dutch Afrikaner homes, for instance, it was often chosen in kitchens because of its supposed capacity to repel flies. If you want to use it in a space that lacks sunshine, team blue with warmer shades such as chocolate brown and pink, which will themselves 'lift' blue tones by introducing their own natural warmth. Of course, even before you start to see the effect of light upon it, it's possible to see which blues are warmer than others. Basically, the more red contained in the mix, the 'warmer' the blue will appear to be. Blue can look both elegant and sophisticated in the home. Navy blue upholstery, for instance, is a classically smart choice in, say, a dining area – but soften it with contrasting stripes, squares or spots in white and, instantly, the look becomes fresher and more relaxed. The combination of navy or sky-blue and white always has an easy breezy charm that lends itself perfectly to holiday and seaside homes.

The combination also works well in home accessories – think of classic blue-and-white willow pattern china. It's unusual, though, to find dining plates that are solid, deep blue in colour – such a strong shade only detracts from what's actually being served. Colour analysts, too, believe that blue can act as an appetite-inhibitor. Others believe that soft blues stimulate intellectual thought, making them a good choice for the study or home office. Some people find the grey tones of blue deeply relaxing, making them excellent for bedrooms. Here, it's important to pay attention to texture: a soft-blue-grey blanket in a marled finish will have a warmer 'feel' – both literally and metaphorically –

# Use blue as either an accent colour or, in a softer shade, let it dominate your décor

**One of the things that makes colour so exciting to work with is the way in which it evokes different responses in different people – and tones that fall within the blue spectrum are certainly no exception. To some, the clarity and natural connotations of blue – blue skies, the sea – mean it resonates as a shade of openness and freedom, redolent of the vast expanses to be found within the natural world.**

Others see blue as a mysterious, velvety colour – think of midnight, or the blue folds of Christ's and the Virgin Mary's robes. It has luxury connotations, too: the first deep and rich shades of blue, made as they were from crushed lapis lazuli, were as costly to produce as they were beautiful to look at. When fading to grey, however, blue can be perceived as a cold, drab colour; depressed Americans even refer to 'feeling blue'. Blue can, of course, be all of these things and none of them. What is a given, though, is that it's a colour that's particularly affected by the natural light it's surrounded by. That's why, in colder, northern-European light, many homemakers avoid it as a shade within living

# The natural world will always prove inspirational when you're looking for your ideal shade of a particular colour

# Yellow
# tones

**Zingy, youthful yellow is an exuberant, life-affirming colour choice in any home. It does need to be used judiciously, though – too much of it in its strongest form can be overpowering. If you're in love with yellow, it's better to stick to pale, creamy tones on walls and floors, and keep sunshine splashes as accent colours on furniture and accessories.**

When thinking of yellow, who can fail to see sunshine, ripening citrus fruits, a child's golden hair, a harvest of corn? It's no wonder this colour is perceived as being both cheering and energising. Its downside, though, is that, despite working so well in the natural world, within our homes it can prove too much of a good thing. For anyone aged over forty, too, it has associations with the 1950s to 1970s, when it was many an interior decorator's colour of choice. That's great if you're looking to create a retro feel in your home, but daunting for those seeking a wholly 21st-century look. As the homes that follow illustrate, however, yellow can look decidedly contemporary if used sparingly and combined with those most elegant of neutrals: black and white. In the home shown left, a room that might otherwise appear too monochrome

and sombre is enlivened with just a short, sharp burst of unexpected yellow – here, in the form of a plastic chair. As an accent colour, it can work particularly well when used in unexpected materials: witness the simple vertical glass window panel shown in this chapter, which allows a syrup-coloured light to stream into the room, and the pared-down blinds in the home illustrated overleaf. Again, these work with natural light to infuse it with soft colour – one that's picked up elsewhere in the room by the trimming on the daybed's bolsters. The overall effect in this space is one of subtlety and sophistication – a far cry from the attention-grabbing properties one might usually associate with yellow. Elsewhere, though, it can be a case of, 'who dares, wins'. Teaming acidic yellow with a shocking pink-red sofa makes ultimate in dramatic statements, yet here the look is prevented from seeming too extreme by the addition of a large monochrome townscape on the wall, a simple glass and chrome table and the dark colour of the floor. Yellow has classic connotations, too: vivid, Chinese yellow – so called because it was the colour of the Imperial family of China – was a popular choice in 19th-century drawing rooms of British country houses and, when teamed with a room's grand proportions and classic antique furniture, can still look extremely elegant today. Because of its warmth and light-enhancing properties, yellow can make an excellent choice for north-facing living rooms. However, go easy if you use it in a bedroom – opt for softer, more restful shades, rather than the acidic ones that are un-likely to promote sleep. It's another colour that's considered to be stimulating, so use it in any space where you're likely to be working – or perhaps in a dining area if you enjoy lively conversations at mealtimes!

The secret to making yellow work in your home – as with all colour – is to stick to shades you truly love, and either use it in modera-tion or team it with other colours that complement it. Soft greens, browns and neutral shades all work well if you're after a restful look; for the ultimate energising effect, team it with equally warm shades of orange, red and pink.

# A splash of yellow will enliven any space

# Red
# tones

**One only has to think of the phrase, 'seeing red' to conjure up images of strong reactions: anger, hot-headedness and passion. Then there are, of course, the communist associations, too. Whatever springs to mind when red's around, one thing is for sure: it's not a colour for the faint-hearted. Used with confidence and conviction, though, it makes a literally brilliant addition to any home's colour scheme, adding warmth and glamour to spaces, whatever their size or style.**

Traditionally associated with good luck in China and with bridal robes in India, red is a primary colour that evokes particularly strong reactions. In the home, it works best as an accent, although – as a supposed appetite-stimulant – it can work well in greater quantities in kitchens and dining areas. Remember, however, that strong colour when used extensively will always make spaces appear smaller – something that can of course be a real asset when you're looking to create a sense of intimacy. Talking of which, in the Chinese system of Feng Shui, red is associated with sexual desire, so it might make a useful choice for anyone wishing to inject a little boudoir spirit into a bedroom... Red lends itself particularly well to shiny finishes: think of Chinese lacquer and gloss paint, both of which can easily be incorporated into the home.

In the homes shown both left and above, we see red being used as an accent colour on window and door frames, while being kept firmly in check through its teaming with more subdued shades of grey. Both colours benefit from the partnership: the grey living room would have looked far too austere without the addition of hot red, while too much red in this room would have been overwhelming.

Red looks both chic and formal when combined with glossy black and white: whether it's used as an accent on the cushion covers of a set of white tulip Eero Saarinen chairs, on the handles of a black wooden cabinet or, as shown on the previous page, combined with the black exterior of a freestanding bath. This shot shows just how well red can work when used in an unexpected setting, and, because it's been used sparingly, it's a good way of providing a visual link between various rooms within the home, too. If a space is sufficiently large and light-filled enough to take it, wall-to-wall red can look terrific, as the photo left proves. Part of the key to the success of this space lies in the fact that red is used in a matt rather than gloss finish: the plasterwork has an earthy sheen, while the large floor tiles are unpolished. Lack of gloss means that the overall effect is warm and enveloping – too much shine and the room would have felt brittle, intimidating and too self-consciously sophisticated. As it is, though, this café feels both inviting and relaxed.

While red is so strong in its own right, it takes on a whole new identity depending on the colours that it's combined with. Sticking to neutral colours within any space it's used in, for instance, means that the accent shade really can come into its own. Paired with black, white, grey or silver, for example, red has a wholly contemporary, smart feel. Team it with purple, ochre and vivid green – as shown within this chapter – and it assumes a rustic, spicy identity that's only intensified by the addition of a rough plasterwork finish on the walls and hand-woven textiles. Alternatively, simply combining red with its primary stablemates of yellow and blue (a primary colour being one that exists only in its own right and thatcannot be created by combining other shades) will bring a youthful, Mondrianesque feel to any room. It makes a good choice for anyone who wants to bring colour into their home, but is keen to avoid a complicated decorative scheme.

If you would like to introduce red into your own home but are unsure where to start, accessories are your answer. And, although these can include everything from cushions and curtains to pottery and glass, perhaps the solution in the first instance is – yet again – to take inspiration from the natural world. A bowl of ripe tomatoes in a white china bowl or a pot of chillies balanced on a kitchen windowsill could lend your space just that flash of vibrant, unmissable colour that you've been waiting for...

# In confident hands, wall-to-wall red can look terrific

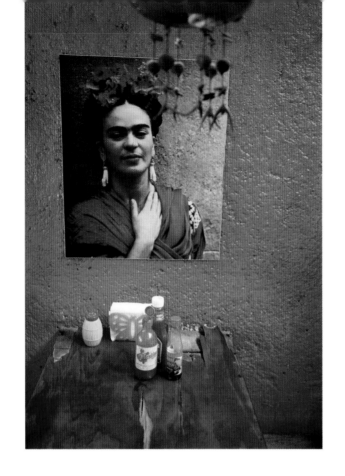

# Combine spicy red with blue, purple, green and ochre for a relaxed and rustic look

Pink
tones

**Back in the early 1980s, Dr. Alexander Schauss reported that a shade he termed Baker-Miller pink had had a noticeable effect on reducing aggression in prisoners. Since that time, while still undisputedly regarded as a colour that will always appeal to the little girl in many of us, there's been no escaping the awareness of pink's calming, restful properties. This is no mere myth: Dr Schauss's thorough research is there to back it up.**

If pink is a colour you adore, though, how best to make it work within the 21st-century home? It's a flamboyant option and, as such, deserves to be used flamboyantly. That's why it works so well in schemes where extravagance, opulence and kitsch are the order of the day. But, while bubblegum pink may be an acquired taste, remember that pink means everything from the softest rose shades to decidedly more adult crushed-raspberry colours. A shocking pink, for instance, when teamed with glossy black, can take on an extremely sophisticated tone. Similarly, temper it with plenty of white and the result can be far from overpowering. Best of all, go to town when using it as an accent colour;

the insides of cupboard doors, kitchen units and alcoves can all benefit from the energising presence of a splash of hot pink, and such spaces are unlikely to be overwhelmed. Use it to emphasise, for example, just a set of suitcases that, when stacked together, serve as storage as well as creating a visual statement. When it comes to throwing other colours into the mix, either stick to neutral browns, creams and greys, or opt for clashing shades of lime green or orange. Again, used in moderation and with confidence, a room should be able to take the unexpected addition of, say, a citrus-hued cushion or green lampshade. If you do want to use a variety of clashing colours without creating a kitsch

# Pink can be used in quantity and still look elegant

**Back in the early 1980s, Dr. Alexander Schauss reported that a shade he termed Baker-Miller pink had had a noticeable effect on reducing aggression in prisoners. Since that time, while still undisputedly regarded as a colour that will always appeal to the little girl in many of us, there's been no escaping the awareness of pink's calming, restful properties. This is no mere myth: Dr Schauss's thorough research is there to back it up.**

If pink is a colour you adore, though, how best to make it work within the 21st-century home? It's a flamboyant option and, as such, deserves to be used flamboyantly. That's why it works so well in schemes where extravagance, opulence and kitsch are the order of the day. But, while bubblegum pink may be an acquired taste, remember that pink means everything from the softest rose shades to decidedly more adult crushed-raspberry colours. A shocking pink, for instance, when teamed with glossy black, can take on an extremely sophisticated tone. Similarly, temper it with plenty of white and the result can be far from overpowering. Best of all, go to town when using it as an accent colour;

the insides of cupboard doors, kitchen units and alcoves can all benefit from the energising presence of a splash of hot pink, and such spaces are unlikely to be overwhelmed. Use it to emphasise, for example, just a set of suitcases that, when stacked together, serve as storage as well as creating a visual statement. When it comes to throwing other colours into the mix, either stick to neutral browns, creams and greys, or opt for clashing shades of lime green or orange. Again, used in moderation and with confidence, a room should be able to take the unexpected addition of, say, a citrus-hued cushion or green lampshade.

# Then again, pink's perfect for a kitsch look...

# ...it can have simple charm, too

# Muted tones

**Toned-down colours – think purple dimmed to lilac, green softened to pistachio – are ideal choices in the home for anyone who loves colour, but relishes a calm, laid-back environment. As the word 'muted' suggests, these are shades that whisper rather than shout, which provide an ideal backdrop to more striking accessories such as furniture and paintings. As such, they can – and do – work a subtle, understated magic on each and every room of the home.**

**S**ome of the prettiest shades to be found within the muted spectrum are the ice-cream, sugared-almond colours that we think of as pastels. Their charm and softness gives them decidedly child-like, feminine overtones, which is why they work so well in spaces such as nurseries and boudoirs. When combined with shabby-chic furniture and retro fabrics, they have a vintage allure that should appeal to nostalgia-lovers everywhere. With pastel colours, one of the most important things to avoid is an overly whimsical or twee look. It is best to break up shades, either by choosing paint effects and finishes that are in sharp contrast to their prettiness – there's nothing 'pretty', for instance, about the unfinished green-painted

plaster wall shown previously – or by combining them with organic materials such as wood (tongue and groove always looks particularly effective when painted in pastel shades) and ironwork. Try to keep any accessories to a minimum, too, and plump for simple, unstructured shapes and designs if you want to avoid fussiness. On the other hand, it is of course entirely down to what works for you: a riot of frilly cushions in pale-green and peach tones could be just what you're after if you're deliberately aiming for an over-the-top kitsch look. Add a few hard edges in the form of steel accessories, contemporary art and furniture, however, and it's possible to transform muted tones into shades that provide an equally effective backdrop to

# Keep shapes simple to avoid a twee look

**Toned-down colours – think purple dimmed to lilac, green softened to pistachio – are ideal choices in the home for anyone who loves colour, but relishes a calm, laid-back environment. As the word 'muted' suggests, these are shades that whisper rather than shout, which provide an ideal backdrop to more striking accessories such as furniture and paintings. As such, they can – and do – work a subtle, understated magic on each and every room of the home.**

**S**ome of the prettiest shades to be found within the muted spectrum are the ice-cream, sugared-almond colours that we think of as pastels.

Their charm and softness gives them decidedly child-like, feminine overtones, which is why they work so well in spaces such as nurseries and boudoirs. When combined with shabby-chic furniture and retro fabrics, they have a vintage allure that should appeal to nostalgia-lovers everywhere. With pastel colours, one of the most important things to avoid is an overly whimsical or twee look. It is best to break up shades, either by choosing paint effects and finishes that are in sharp contrast to their prettiness – there's nothing 'pretty', for instance, about the unfinished green-painted plaster wall shown previously – or by combining them with organic materials such as wood (tongue and groove always looks particularly effective when painted in pastel shades) and ironwork. Try to keep any accessories to a minimum, too, and plump for simple, unstructured shapes and designs if you want to avoid fussiness. On the other hand, it is of course entirely down to what works for you: a riot of frilly cushions in pale-green and peach tones could be just what you're after if you're deliberately aiming for an over-the-top kitsch look.

Add a few hard edges in the form of steel accessories, contemporary art and furniture, however, and it's possible to transform muted tones into shades that provide an equally effective backdrop to a more masculine, contemporary style of living.

Away from the pastels, there is a wealth of muted tones that are ideal for bringing sophisticated, serene style to living spaces. Beige, taupe and even the much-maligned magnolia can be enlivened with stronger colour to create the best of both worlds.

le renversement de

# Muted shades evoke a sense of restfulness

# Brown
# tones

**Chocolate, nuts, coffee, toffee – who doesn't think of shades of brown and feel their mouth water? This is a colour that manages to be rich and sophisticated and yet down-to-earth as well. In many ways, it's the perfect choice of colour for nature-loving home-makers, simply because it's found in such abundance in the trees, leaves and soil of the natural world. It's a colour that lends itself perfectly to creating spaces with a cocooning, nurturing feel.**

In many ways, brown is the easiest of colours to introduce to the home – simply add wooden furniture, and you've made a start already. And because wood comes in every possible shade, finish and texture, and with the endless variations of grain a sure-fire way to add interest to every surface, you've got a virtually limitless range of browns to choose from even if you confine yourself to a wood-filled room. Add plastics, the lustre of metallic golds, coppers and bronze, though, and the brown-toned home can take on the most glamorous of finishes.

When it comes to paintwork, solid brown walls add a sense of intimacy to a space, and take on a luxurious feel in, say, a living room when partnered with touchy-feely sheepskin rugs and cream velvet throws over sofas and chairs. Add a log fire and you've got the perfect, laid-back bolt-hole for winter. Alternatively, create a retro feel with 60s-style teak furniture in caramel tones, or keep it contemporary by choosing sustainable wenge or iroko wood for kitchen cabinets. Traditionalists, meanwhile, will love the chestnut-brown shades found in old leather clubhouse sofas and mahogany antiques. Just add some classic-framed prints or sepia-toned photos for a look that could have come straight out of a Ralph Lauren catalogue...

# Rich shades of brown can look good enough to eat

# Green tones

**Of all the colours in the spectrum, it's arguably green that prompts the strongest associations. Grass, leaves, sap, deep pools within the sea – the verdant natural world is instantly what springs to mind. Yet, for all its natural connotations, green can be one of the trickiest colours to make work within the home. Too little of it and it can look wishy-washy, too much and rooms can appear as if they would be better suited to outdoor than indoor living.**

To make green work within the home, it's vital to choose the right shade of green. A rich olive, for instance, will work better in cool northern-European light than the sort of pale, chlorophyll-inspired shade that can prove so refreshing in hot climates. If you choose a rich green, however, go easy – perhaps in the first instance applying it only to a feature wall and toning it down with plenty of contrasting neutrals such as soft stone or white. Another way to break up solid blocks of colour is by using patterned fabric that incorporates the green of your choice, but that also contains plenty of refreshing white. Remember, too, that vivid green

– the sort of almost-luminous colour that you don't actually tend to see in nature – will create a retro feel, so use it sparingly as an accent, on door frames or the odd piece of vintage furniture for instance. The easiest greens to live with are the softer shades: think restful sage, which you can team with other natural colours as well as with natural materials such as linen, cotton and seagrass.

If it's watery, sea-greens that you crave for your home, either play it safe by using them in smaller spaces with appropriately watery themes – the bathroom and kitchen – or introduce it via accessories from cushions in eau de nil silk to delicate Japanese pottery.

# Soft greens
# are soothing...

# ...while vivid greens can have a retro feel

# Natural tones

**Natural tones take their inspiration from the soft shades of sand, stone and shell. They work brilliantly when teamed with organic materials – seagrass, wood or stone flooring, crafts-men-made bespoke furniture, hand-thrown pottery. Homes that make the most of the natural colour palette tend to be informal spaces that blur the boundaries between indoor and outdoor living. The result is a look that's relaxed, laid back and very easy to live in.**

If you're someone who wants to create a timeless backdrop for their lifestyle, natural tones are the ideal colour choice for you. Stone-coloured walls, for instance, are easy to live with and won't date, so you won't have to think about redecorating on a regular basis – instead, you can just get on with the business of living in your home.

Natural colours are unobtrusive and restful – perfect for any home that's a sanctuary for busy people. Moreover, if you're looking for inspiration when it comes to putting together your colour scheme, you've only got to walk along any beach to find that the combination of pebbles, sand and driftwood prove a great starting point.

Accessorise any home featuring natural colours with simple shapes and tactile, organic materials. Steer away from anything synthetic and instead think wood, straw, raffia and stone. Not only will these add texture and interest to the calming setting you've created, their soft, worn-away colours should also provide a good complement to whatever shade of paint you've chosen for your walls. Then add simple furniture of wood and raffia into the mix for an understated look that's as timeless as it is comforting and comfortable.

# Natural equals restful

# Natural tones are an ideal choice for the 'lived-in' look

# Credits

**Front cover**
Photographer Nathalie Krag
Producer Tami Christiansen

**P 5, 6, 7, 8, 12, 13, 16-17 middle, 18, 19,
28, 29, 34-35 middle, 36, 48, 50, 51, 53,
55, 56, 59, 62, 63, 70, 71, 72-73, 73, 78,
84, 85, 90, 91 middle**
Photographer Mikkel Vang

**P 10, 72, 92**
Photographer Earl Carter
Producer Annemarie Kiely

**P 11, 34**
Photographer Nathalie Krag
Producer Letitzia Donati

**P 14, 57**
Photographer Nathalie Krag
Producer Helene Schjerbeck

**P 15, 89**
Photographer Mikkel Vang
Producer Christine Rudolph

**P 16**
Photographer Hans Zeegers

**P 17, 24, 25, 31, 46, 66 and 66-67 middle,
77, 82-83 middle, 83, 86**
Photographer Nathalie Krag
Producer Tami Christiansen

**P 20**
Photographer Marjon Hoogervorst
Producer Tatjana Quax

**P 21, 22, 23, 45, 49**
Photographer and producer Ngoc Minh Ngo

**P 26, 27, 30, 35, 42, 58, 88, 88-89 middle**
Photographer Karina Tengberg
Producer Tami Christiansen

**P 32, 80, 81, 82**
Photographer Ben Lambers
Producer Tatjana Quax

**P 37, 38, 39, 40, 67, 87, 91, 93**
Photographer Anne Dokter
Producer Stella Willing

**P 41, 44**
Photographer Wilfried Overwater
Producer Rosa Lisa

**P 43, 64**
Photographer Prue Ruscoe
Producer Andrea Millar

**P 46-47**
Photographer Prue Ruscoe
Producer Megan Morton

**P 52, 90, 94, 95**
Photographer Matthew Williams

**P 60**
Photographer Pablo Benitez
Producer Matias Errazuriz

**P 61**
Photographer Jim Hensley
Producer Nina Dreyer

**P 65**
Photographer Mikkel Heriba
Producer Christine Rudolph

**P 68, 69**
Photographer Prue Ruscoe
Producer Amanda Mahoney

**P 74, 75**
Photographer Ditte Isager
Producer Christine Rudolph

**P 76**
Photographer Hotze Eisma
Producer Maarten Spruyt

**P 79**
Photographer John Dummer
Producer Yvonne Bakker